Crochet WIRE JEWELRY

Nancy Waille

Thank you to the Weber Métaux and Table et Deco societies, who kindly supplied me with the wire I needed for developing and making the creations in the book. Thank you also to Nancy Chabert and MOKUBA society for their wonderful ribbons.

I thank Colette Hanicotte for her confidence and enthusiasm, as well as Natalia Dobiecka.

Published by
STACKPOLE BOOKS
5067 Ritter Road
Mechanicsburg, PA 17055
www.stackpolebooks.com

Printed in Romania

10 9 8 7 6 5 4 3 2 1

First edition
French edition originally published by Dessain et Tolra/Larousse in 2009

Library of Congress Cataloging-in-Publication Data
Waille, Nancy.
  [Bijoux en maille metal au crochet. English]
  Crochet wire jewelry / Nancy Waille. — 1st ed.
     p. cm.
  ISBN 978-0-8117-1054-1
  1. Crocheting. 2. Wire. 3. Jewelry making. I. Title.
  TT820.W12513 2011
  746.43'4—dc23
                          2011012259

Stackpole Books
Translation: Kathryn Fulton
Pagination: Tessa Sweigert
Dessain et Tolra/Larousse
Editorial management: Colette Hanicotte, assisted by Natalia Dobiecka and Anna Stroganova
Graphic design and pagination: Violette Bénilan
Photography and design: Cactus studio
Photos of materials by Olivier Ploton
Fabrication: Anne Raynaud

Crochet WIRE JEWELRY

Nancy Waille

STACKPOLE
BOOKS

Collier — Plastron

Contents

Materials

Crochet is a craft that needs very few tools. The materials on these pages are all you'll need to make all the creations presented in this book.

Wire

The wire used for crochet is quite varied: brass wire, annealed copper wire, enameled copper wire, aluminum wire, stainless steel wire. You can find it on spools, sold by length or weight, in different gauges.

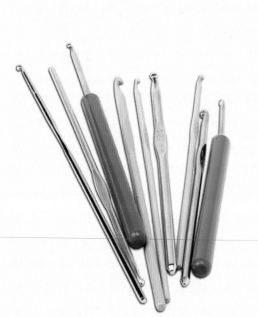

Crochet hooks

Crochet hooks can be made from many materials: aluminum, steel, wood, or plastic. They are available in varying sizes, which allows you to make larger or smaller stitches. I used hooks in sizes B, C, D, E, G, and H to make the jewelry in this book, but don't hesitate to change the size of the hook you're using if the size I used isn't working for you.

Other tools...

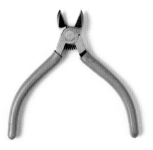

Pliers with wire cutters, which will replace scissors

A hammer to flatten out the work (see page 15)

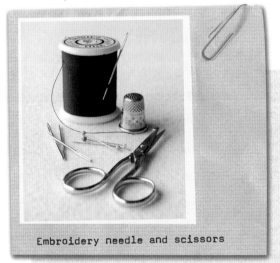

Embroidery needle and scissors

Fabric, ribbons, cords, and so on

Sewing thread and embroidery thread

Materials and tools for these projects are available at craft stores, sewing shops, or through online retailers.

Crochet basics

Crochet consists of seven basic stitches: chain stitch, slip stitch, single crochet, half double crochet, double crochet, treble crochet, and double treble crochet.

Hand position

First, you need to learn how to hold the hook. There are two ways of holding the crochet hook (shown here in the right hand):

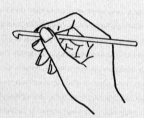

like a pencil...

or like a fork.

You will hold the wire with your other hand. Guide it with your index finger.

Key to the stitch charts

o	chain	T (double crochet symbol)	double crochet
.	slip stitch	(treble crochet symbol)	treble crochet
+	single crochet	(double treble symbol)	double treble crochet
±	single crochet (worked in the back loop only)	(3 together symbol)	work 3 double crochet together
T	half-double crochet		

Chain stitch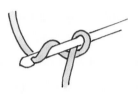

1 Start by making a slip knot: Form a loop with the end of your wire, leaving a few inches hanging down. Slide the hook through this loop. Yarn over (catch the wire coming from the spool with your hook). Then bring the yard through the loop, pulling the hook from left to right. Gently tighten the slip knot on the hook.

2 Yarn over, as illustrated here.
   Bring a loop through the slip knot.

3 Repeat step 2 the desired number of times, moving your left hand progressively so that you are holding the chain just below the hook.

Slip stitch •

1 On a chain, insert the hook through the second stitch from the hook. On a piece of two or more rows, insert the hook through the top of the stitch as indicated in the instructions. In either case, yarn over next and bring the wire through both loops at once.

Single crochet +

On a chain, insert the hook into the second stitch from the hook. On a work in progress, insert the hook into the top of the stitch indicated, then:

<u>1</u> Yarn over and bring the wire through the stitch, as shown here.

<u>2</u> Yarn over again and bring the wire through two loops. At the end of the row, chain one to turn.

Half double crochet T

<u>1</u> On a chain, yarn over once and insert the hook into the third stitch from the hook. Yarn over and pull the wire through the stitch.

<u>2</u> You should have three loops on the hook. Yarn over once and bring the wire through the three loops.

After the last stitch, chain two and turn. Then start the first half double crochet of the next row in the second stitch from the hook.

Double crochet ⊤

1 On a chain, yarn over once and insert the hook into the fourth stitch from the hook. On a work in progress, yarn over once and insert the hook into the top of the stitch indicated. Yarn over again and pull the wire through the stitch.

2 Yarn over and bring the wire through the first two loops.

3 Yarn over again and bring the wire through the remaining two loops.

At the end of the row, chain three to turn. Then start the first double crochet of the next row in the second stitch from the hook.

Treble crochet ‡

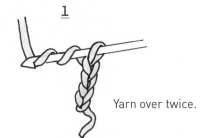

1

Yarn over twice.

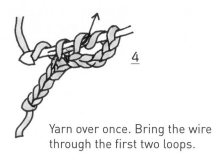

2

Insert the hook into the fifth chain from the hook, then yarn over.

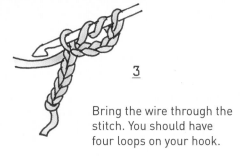

3

Bring the wire through the stitch. You should have four loops on your hook.

4

Yarn over once. Bring the wire through the first two loops.

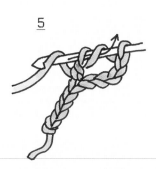

5

Yarn over again and bring the wire through the next two loops.

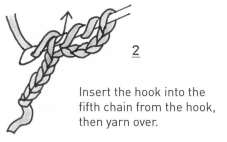

6

Yarn over one last time and bring the wire through the last two loops.

At the end of the row, chain four to turn. Then begin the first treble crochet of the next row in the second stitch from the hook.

Double treble crochet

1 On a chain, begin with three yarn overs, then follow steps 2 through 6 for treble crochet, with these variations: In step 2 insert the hook into the sixth stitch from the hook, and work step 5 twice. Chain 5 to turn.

2 The completed stitch.

Double crochet two together

1 Make three incomplete double crochets, without the third step. Yarn over and bring the wire through all four loops on the hook.

2 The finished stitch.

Tips and tricks

Crocheting with wire made of real metal, such as copper, brass, and stainless steel, involves a few particular cautions.

- Crocheting involves twisting the wire or yarn used. As a result, the two sides of the work will look different. When you assemble several pieces together, look at the work and place all the pieces with the same side up to avoid this difference in texture between different pieces in a project.

- Unlike the yarn usually used for crocheting, wire retains the memory of the movement it's been put through, and it is hard to bring it back to its original shape. For example, if you make a fold in the wire in the course of working, you will not be able to get rid of it entirely, even if you pull it; a little bump, like a scar, will remain forever. It's equally difficult to unravel your work; you won't be able to unravel many more than one or two stitches, because the wire will come out damaged. You will then have to be careful that these little bumps don't block the movement of the wire in the next stitch.

- Crochet stitches in wire are irregular, which is completely normal. As a result, it's sometimes difficult to distinguish the stitches in the work. So take the time to study it carefully and if necessary use a sewing needle (with a blunt point so you don't hurt yourself) to pick up the strand of the stitch that the hook needs to go under. This is also why in many of the projects in this book I suggest inserting the hook in only one of the two loops of the little chain on the top of each stitch; it's easier than having to pick up both strands, and the result is lighter.

- Use your fingers to shape or even out a shape while you are working on it.

- If you're not very sure of yourself, make a practice piece: First crochet the object you're making with yarn—cotton or wool, it doesn't matter.

- Like you usually do when crocheting, hold the wire at the beginning while you crochet the first stitches. At the end of the work, before cutting the wire with the wire cutters, weave it into the backside of the work with an embroidery needle (its eye will damage the wire less than that of a sewing needle). In some cases, however, you shouldn't weave the wire in right away but instead cut it off, leaving a sufficient length for assembling the pieces with small stitches with the embroidery needle (or sewing needle).

- Flattening out cloth crocheted in wire reveals its beauty. When you have finished a piece, place it on a magazine or a piece of felt; put a second piece of felt or a magazine (not too thick) on top and tap the entire area where the crocheted piece is with a hammer. Turn the piece over and slide it between the two magazines or pieces of felt again and tap it with the hammer again. The metal "lace" will appear, fixed and rigid. You can then, if necessary, assemble the piece. Only the spherical earrings and ring are not flattened, just shaped by hand.

Abbreviations

The patterns for making the pieces in this book use abbreviations. Here is the list that will allow you to understand the steps in the patterns.

ch = chain

dc = double crochet

dc2tog = double crochet 2 together

dec = decrease

dtr = double treble

hdc = half double crochet

in = inches

mm = millimeters

sc = single crochet

sk = skip

sl st = slip stitch

st(s) = stitch(es)

tog = together

tr = treble crochet

. = repeat the action between the asterisks the number of times indicated.
Ch x = make a chain (x) stitches long.

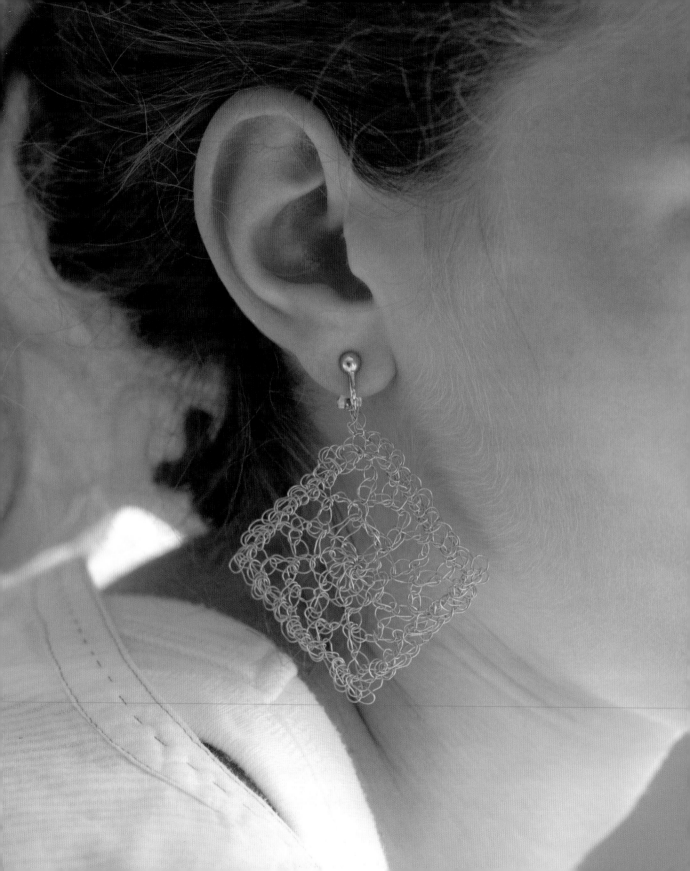

Rings, brooches,
and earrings

Sphere earrings and ring

This single sphere pattern makes two pieces of jewelry: Keep it three-dimensional and fill it for the earrings, and flatten it out for the ring.

Materials

For the earrings:

1 spool of 29-gauge wire in the color of your choice

Ear wires or other earring components

A bit of wool or cotton a matching color

Size B/2.00 mm crochet hook

For the ring:

2 spools of 29-gauge wire in two different colors (e.g. apple green and red or lavender and orange)

Embroidery needle

Size B/2.00 mm crochet hook

Making the ring

- The cabochon: Crochet rounds 1 to 5 with the first color, then skip to rounds 8 and 9 (the top of the ring), working these rounds in the contrasting color. Thread the remaining wire in the needle and slide it through the back strands of the eight stitches of the last row. Pull to gather and close up the ball; weave the wire in and cut off the excess. Shape and crush the ball by hand, then flatten it out with the hammer.

- The ring band: Make a chain in the first color the size of your finger—here, 17 stitches plus 1 to turn—and return, working 1 sc in each of the 17 stitches. Then turn with one chain and work down the other side of the chain, still in sc. Leave a length of wire, flatten this rectangle, then sew it under the cabochon, closing it up to form a ring. Weave in the wire and cut it off.

Making the earrings

These earrings are crocheted in the round, which means the pattern is in rounds rather than rows.

- Start with a central loop, crocheting in the back loop of each stitch from the second round on. Close each round with a slip stitch, then chain one to go to the next round.

  Round 1: 8 sc (see the instructions on the opposite page)
  Round 2: [2 sc in each st] 8x = 16 st
  Round 3: [1 sc in the first st, 2 sc in the next st] 8x = 24 st
  Round 4, 5, 6, and 7: 24 st
  Round 8: [2 sc, sk 1 st] 8x = 16 st
  Round 9: [1 sc, sk 1 st] = 8 st

- Put a bit of wool or cotton into the ball, stuffing it well. Then make one last round of 2 or 3 sc and 1 slip stitch to close it up. Save a short length of wire which you will slide into the end of the ear wires, or make an arch of 4 ch and 1 sl st on the top of the ball and slide that into the ear wires.

- No flattening for the earrings!

Working in the round

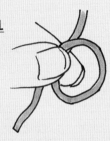

1

Bend the end of the wire into a circle and hold it in your left hand.

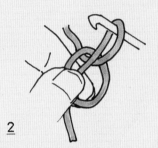

2

Yarn over with the wire coming from the spool and bring it through the circle.

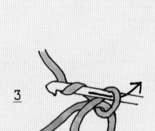

3

Yarn over and pull the wire through the loop to make a chain stitch.

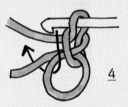

4

The chain stitch will stand in for the height of a single crochet.

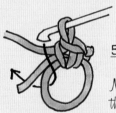

5

Now work the number of single crochets specified through the circle, crocheting around the end of the wire as well.

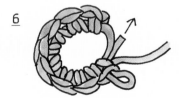

6

Pull the end in the direction of the arrow in this drawing to close the circle.

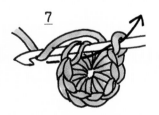

7

At the end of the round, close the row with a slip stitch.

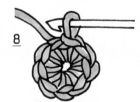

8

The first row of eight single crochets is finished.

Cubist brooch

In shades of red or green, four single crochet rectangles compose this easy-to-make brooch.

Materials

1 spool of 29-gauge wire in each color:

Fuschia, red, pink, and lavender (red brooch) or

Mint green, champagne, apple green, and turquoise (green brooch)

Pin back

Embroidery needle

Size B/2.00 mm crochet hook

Making the brooch

- All the pieces are worked in single crochet.

  A = small square, about 1¼ x 1¼ in: chain 10 + 1 to turn, and crochet 9 rows.
  B = large square, about 2 x 2 in: chain 14 + 1 to turn, and crochet 14 rows.
  C = large rectangle, about 1 x 2¾ in: chain 7 + 1 to turn and crochet 20 rows.
  D = narrow rectangle, about ½ x 2½ in: chain 4 + 1 to turn and crochet 17 rows.
  Red brooch: crochet A in fuschia, B in red, C in pink, and D in lavender.
  Green brooch: crochet A in mint green, B in champagne, C in apple green, and D in turquoise.

- Leave the leftover lengths of wire for assembling the project. Flatten all the pieces.

Assembling the brooch

- Following the diagram, place C on top of B and sew them together with the remaining wire from C; then sew A onto C with the remnant of A; then sew D onto A and B.

- Weave all wires in except for one or two in colors A or D. Flatten the four assembled pieces again. Sew the pin back onto the back with the remaining lengths of wire, putting the needle through all four squares.

Diagram for assembling
the brooch

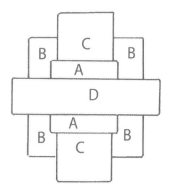

Red hearts

Brooch or pendant, the pattern is the same; just change the thickness of the wire. This piece could also be put on a tote bag or be used as a keychain.

Materials

For the brooch:

20 grams (approximately) of 24-gauge red enamelled copper wire

A pin back

Size G/4.00 mm crochet hook

For the pendant:

1 spool of 29-gauge red wire

About 60 in red organdy ribbon, $1/2$ in wide

A bit of wool or angora in a contrasting color

Size D/3.00 mm crochet hook

Making the hearts

- The hearts are worked in single crochet, always with one chain at the end of the row to turn. Follow the pattern below.

A: Ch 3.
  Row 1: 2 sc in second and third chain from hook = 4 sts.
  Row 2: 2 sc in the first st, 1 sc in each of the next 2 sts, 2 sc in the last st = 6 sts. Cut the wire and leave a long end hanging.

B: Work rows 1 and 2 the same as for A, then:
  Row 3: Work across B, then across A: 2 sc in the first st, 1 sc each of the next 10 sts, and 2 sc in the last st = 14 sts.
  Row 4, 5, and 6: 1 sc in each st across = 14 sts.
  Row 7: Dec 1 st at the beginning (sk the first st) and at the end (st the next-to-last st) of the row.
  Row 8: 1 sc in each st across = 12 sts.
  Rows 9, 10, 11, and 12: Row 7.
  Row 13: 1 sc in the second and fourth sts from the hook.
  Row 14: Sc in the second st from the hook. The point of the heart is finished.

Assembly

- Brooch: For the brooch, work the sc are through the back loop of each stitch. Go all the way around the heart in sl st: 20 sts from the point of the heart to the trough between A and B, 1 st in the trough, and 20 sts along the other side to finish at the point. Weave in the ends and cut them.

- Flatten out the heart, then sew the pin back onto the back of the shape.

- Pendant: Cut the wire off, leaving about 15 in. Crochet two identical hearts, flatten them out, and sew them together with the whip stitch. Leave an opening to stuff the shape with wool or angora. Then close it completely. With the remaining wire in the trough between A and B, ch 5, then work 1 sl st in the trough to form a loop through which you can thread the ribbon. Attach it there with a fringe knot (see page 41).

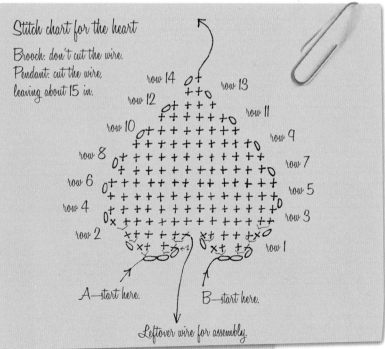

Stitch chart for the heart

Brooch: don't cut the wire.
Pendant: cut the wire, leaving about 15 in.

row 14   row 13
row 12   row 11
row 10   row 9
row 8   row 7
row 6   row 5
row 4   row 3
row 2   row 1

A—start here.   B—start here.

Leftover wire for assembly.

Square earrings

In black or in silver, these earrings are quick to make and very light to wear!

Materials

1 spool of 29-gauge wire in the color of your choice

Ear wires in the same color as the wire

Size C/2.75 mm crochet hook

Making the earrings

• Make 2 squares, following the stitch chart on the opposite page and the pattern below.

• Begin with a loop (see page 21, steps 1 and 2).

Round 1: Ch 3 (counts as first dc), 7 dc, close the round with one sl st.

Round 2: Ch 1, 1 sc on the top of the 3 ch from the previous row, *ch 3, 1 sc in next dc* 7 times, ch 3, 1 sl st to close the round.

Round 3: Ch 5, *1 sc in the arch of the three chains, ch 2* twice, and [1 dc in the sc, ch 2, work the sts between * and * twice] 3 times, and 1 sl st to close the round.

Round 4: Ch 1, then 1 sc in each st of round 3 except for the corners. In each corner dc of round 3, work 1 sc, ch 1, 1 sc. Finish the round with a sl st, then make a loop of 4 ch and 1 sl st to close it.

• After weaving the ends into the work, cut them and flatten out the piece.

Assembly

• Slide or sew the loop into the ear wires.

Stitch chart

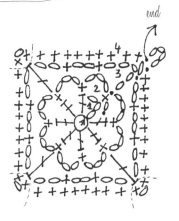

end

Necklaces
and bracelets

Pendant with three disks

Three disks in decreasing sizes mix shades of green with black for a pendant that will not go unnoticed.

Materials

1 spool of 29-gauge mint green varnished wire

1 spool of 29-gauge apple green varnished wire

1 spool of 29-gauge turquoise varnished wire

1 spool of 29-gauge black varnished wire

65 in satin ribbon, 0.1 in wide

40 in satin ribbon, 0.4 in wide

Size E/3.75 mm crochet hook

Making the pendant

Each disk is crocheted with two strands of wire. They are worked in sc through the back loop of each stitch, as explained on page 63.

- Small circle: Crochet together one strand mint green and one strand black, for 3 rounds, then ch 5 and work 1 sl st in the first of the five ch to close the ring. Cut the wire, leaving about 6 in.

- Medium circle: Crochet together one strand apple green and one strand black, for 5 rounds. Cut the wire, leaving about 6 in.

- Large circle: Crochet together one strand turquoise and one strand black, for 7 rounds, then ch 5 and work 1 sl st in the first of the five ch to close the ring. Cut the wire off at 3 in.

- Weave in the remaining wire on the large circle only, and cut off the end. Flatten out the three circles.

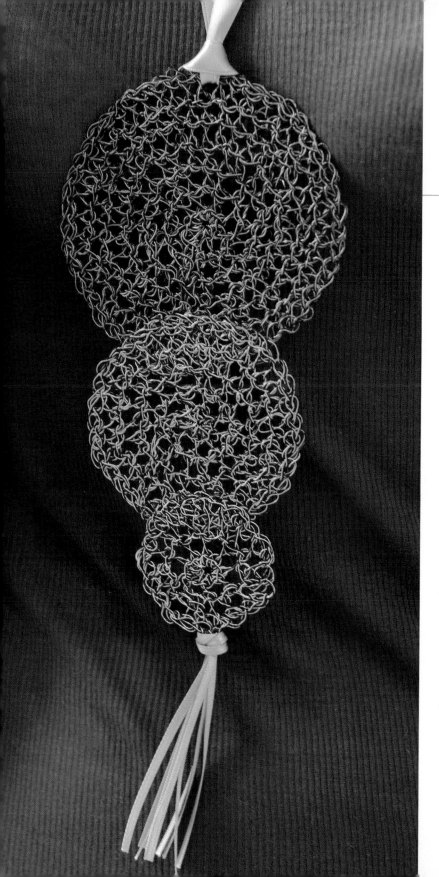

Assembly

- Overlap the medium circle over the large one and attach it by sewing the pieces together with the remaining length of wire. Placing it with the small loop pointing down, overlap the small circle over the bottom of the medium one in the same way, making sure the centers of the three circles are lined up, and sew it to the medium one. Weave in and cut the ends of the wire. Flatten out the work again.

- Fold the length of 0.4-in ribbon in half. Slide it through the top of the large circle, from the front to the back, in line with the centers of the circles. Then make a fringe knot with it.

- Cut the narrow ribbon into eight lengths of 8 in each and slide them together through the ring at the bottom of the pendant in a fringe knot. Even out the lengths.

- Tie the pendant around your neck and, if necessary, cut off the extra ribbon.

Petal collar

Collar and necklace at the same time, this piece will delicately dress up an outfit. Change the length of the necklace and the number of petals according to your taste; this piece will be equally beautiful in black or silver.

Materials

1 spool 29-gauge annealed brass wire

65 in gold metallic ribbon 0.4 in wide

Sewing thread in a matching color

Size D/3.25 mm crochet hook

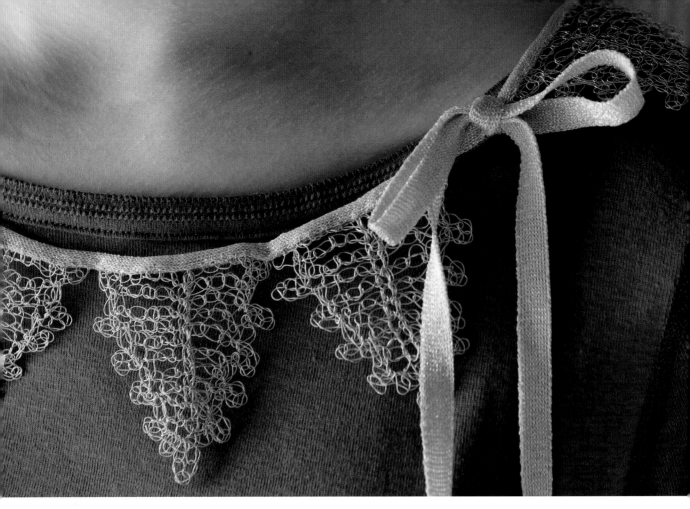

Making the necklace

- Make 11 petals (or fewer for a smaller necklace), following the stitch chart on the next page.

- Ch 10 plus 1 to turn.

  Row 1: 1 sc in each of the 10 ch, turn.

  Row 2: Ch 5 (= 1 dtr), *2 dtr, 2 tr, 2 dc, 2 hdc, 1 sc**, ch 1, 1 sl st in the ch for the point of the petal, ch 1, and on the other side of the foundation row of chains, work from ** back to *, 1 dtr, turn.

  Row 3: ****Ch 3, 1 sc in the last dtr of Row 2, *ch 1, sk 1, 1 sc, ch 3, 1 sc in the same stitch.* Work from * to * 4 times in all, ch 2, *** and in the sl st of the point, 1 sl st, ch 5, 1 sl st, then work the same thing in reverse on the other side of the petal, going from *** to ****, and finishing with 1 sc.

- After weaving in the remaining wire, cut the ends off and flatten the work.

Assembly

- In the middle of the ribbon, place one petal, then add five others on each side, sewing them onto the ribbon with small running stitches in sewing thread along their tops.

- Fold the ribbon in half from top to bottom along the length occupied by the petals and close it with small running stitches to hide the sewing that holds the petals in.

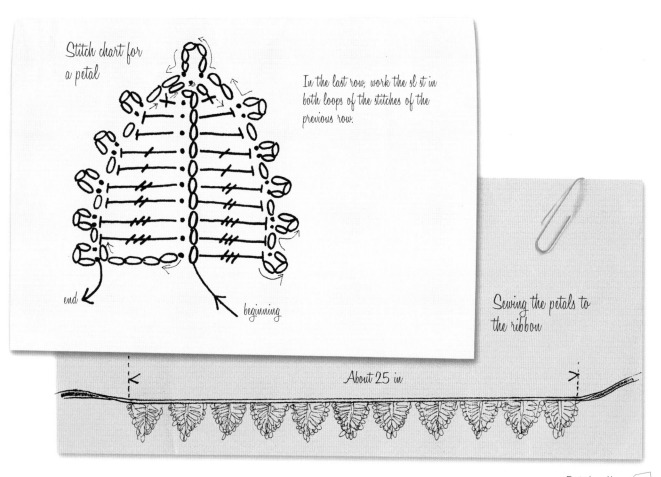

Stitch chart for a petal

In the last row, work the sl st in both loops of the stitches of the previous row.

end

beginning

Sewing the petals to the ribbon

About 25 in

Glamorous choker

Red velvet and black lace—a timeless and unchanging combination.
This choker will also be very seductive made with red wire and
mounted on a black velvet ribbon.

Materials

1 spool of 29-gauge black varnished wire

Approximately 20 in red velvet ribbon 0.6 in wide

A small black button or snap

Black sewing thread

A bit of embroidery floss or thread in the same shade of red as the ribbon

Size B/2.00 mm crochet hook

Making the necklace

Starting with a loop (p. 21, steps 1 and 2), make 3 squares:

• One large square following the entire stitch chart, leaving 6 in of wire to use to sew the pieces together.

• One medium square crocheting only the first two rounds in the diagram (finish the second round with 1 sl st), leaving 6 in of wire again.

• One small square, crocheting only the first round and finishing with 1 sl st. Then on the next side of the square work in each of 6 st [ch 3, 1 sc] to form 6 small loops. Cut and weave in the tail of the wire.

• Flatten out the three squares.

Stitch chart for the
large square

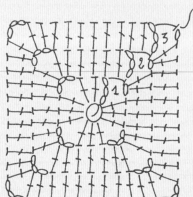

Assembly

- Sew the three squares together (see the diagram below), being careful to place the medium square underneath the large one and the small square underneath the medium one (to hide your stitches); the little loops need to be at the very bottom.

- Attach the strands of embroidery floss or thread to these little loops with a fringe knot (see page 41) and trim the ends.

- Sew the large square to the middle of the ribbon with black sewing thread. Trim the ribbon to fit your neck. In the back, fold over ½ in on each end for the hem. Sew a small button loop on one end with the red thread, and sew the button on the other end.

TIP:
You can replace the button and the loop with a snap. In this case, reserve about ¹/₂ in more ribbon so it can cross over itself.

Assembling the squares

— wire passing under the square

···· running stitch assembling the two squares

Bring the wire to the back once you finish sewing.

ends of the remaining wires from the large and medium squares

Leaf necklace

A cascade of leaves hanging from airy ribbons to romanticize a T-shirt and sweater.

Materials

1 spool of 24-gauge tin-plated copper wire

1 spool of 29-gauge annealed brass wire

1 spool of 24-gauge annealed brass wire

1 spool of 34-gauge annealed stainless steel wire

Approximately 65 in iridescent gray organdy ribbon, 0.6 in wide

Approximately 65 in iridescent champagne organdy ribbon, 0.7 in wide

Size 8/2.00 mm, D/3.25 mm, and G/4.00 mm crochet hooks

1 embroidery needle

TIP: You can make extra leaves for a bushier necklace or for matching earrings.

Making the leaves

For each leaf, follow the diagram:

- Ch 12 plus 1 to turn. Work in these 12 ch: *1 sc, 2 sl st, 2 hdc, 2 dc, 3 tr, 1 dc, and 1 hdc**; ch 3 to turn to the other side of the foundation chain and crochet down the other side from ** back to *. Then work in the chain of the point: 1 sc, working through the back loop, ch 1, 1 sc through the back loop, and continue working sc through the back loops of each of the stitches of the previous row, all the way around the leaf.

- You are at the point again: ch 2, 1 sl st in the chain of the point, and come back to the middle, working 1 sl st in each stitch of the starting chain to form the vein.

- Finish with 5 ch (6 for leaves in the finest wire) and 1 sc at the base of the leaf to form the ring through which you will tie the ribbon(s). Cut the wire.

- Make in this manner:

  1 leaf in 24-gauge tin-plated copper with the size G hook

  1 leaf in 24-gauge annealed brass with the size G hook

  3 leaves in 29-gauge annealed brass 0.3 with the size D hook

  11 leaves in 34-gauge annealed stainless steel 0.16 with the size B hook

- After weaving the ends of the wires into the back of the work with the embroidery needle, cut them with the pliers and flatten out all the leaves.

Assembly

- Fold the two ribbons together in the middle and make a fringe knot (see the diagram below) in the loop of the largest brass leaf. Next, knot the other leaves onto the ribbons, going up from each side of the central leaf without trying for symmetry; arrange them in a very free manner, to achieve the effect of a disorderly fall of leaves. From time to time you can knot only one of the two ribbons onto one of the leaves, if you like. Mix and alternate the large leaves and the small leaves; the highest ones should be the smallest ones so that their weight doesn't make the fall of the necklace unbalanced.

- Knot the ribbons together behind your neck, adjusting to the desired length, and cut off the extra length of ribbon on the bias.

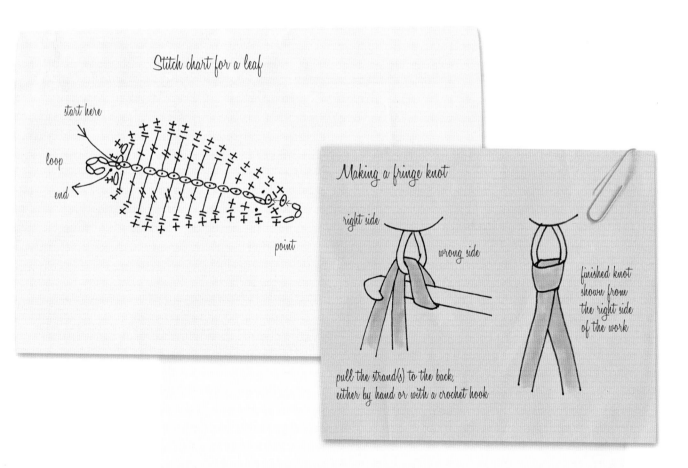

Stitch chart for a leaf

start here

loop

end

point

Making a fringe knot

right side

wrong side

finished knot shown from the right side of the work

pull the strand(s) to the back, either by hand or with a crochet hook

Cluster necklace

A cluster of gold rosettes, very simple to make, form a unique necklace that would be equally beautiful in silver or black.

Materials

50 grams 24-gauge annealed brass wire

60 in (approximately) black vinyl ribbon 0.2 in wide

Size G/4.00 mm and H/5.00 mm crochet hooks

Making the rosettes

- Ch 16 with the size H hook. With the size G hook, close up the ring of 16 ch with a sl st, and in each of the stitches of the circle formed, work 1 sc, ch 3, 1 sc. Close up the row with a sl st. Cut the wire at approximately 8 in, but don't weave it in; you will use it to assemble the piece.

- For the sc, insert the crochet hook through the middle of each chain forming the circle, and not through the circle itself. Don't forget to use the wire leading to the spool when starting the first few stitches with the new hook.

- Make seven rosettes. Flatten them out.

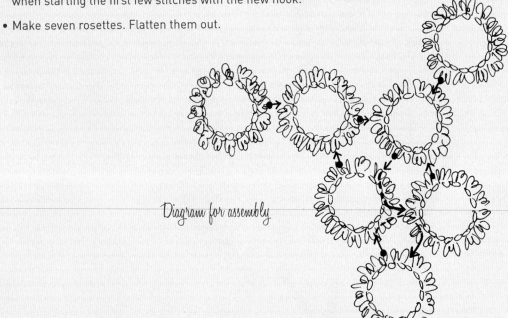

Diagram for assembly

Assembly

- Follow the diagram, which shows where the ending wires from each motif should go; the black dot and arrow represent the placement of the ending wires, where you will make a few tight stitches with the embroidery needle to attach the rosette to the next one. As there are nine places were stitches are needed and only seven ending wires, the dotted lines show the route along the back of the work where some of the wires should go to reach another area where stitches are needed.

- Cut all the woven-in wires and flatten the work one more time.

- Cut the ribbon in half. Fold each of the lengths obtained in half and slide them in a fringe knot (see page 41) through the tops of two motifs.

- Put the necklace on and adjust the lengths of the ribbons to your neck.

TIP:
Try making up your
own arrangement of
the rosettes.

Cuff bracelet

It spectacularly covers
the wrist while staying
light and comfortable.
It would also be very
beautiful in black,
bordered in gold or
silver.

Materials

1 spool 24-gauge burgundy enameled copper wire

1 spool 29-gauge red enameled copper wire

1 button

Red sewing thread

Size D/3.25 mm and G/4.00 mm crochet hooks

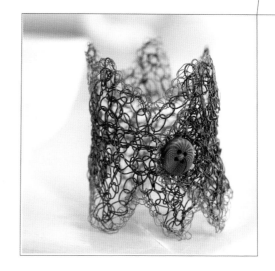

Making the bracelet

Follow the stitch chart:

- With the burgundy wire and the size G hook, chain 23 plus 1 to turn, and go back in sc, then work *ch 1, 1 sl st, ch 1* to turn and work in sc down the other side of the chain of 23 sts. Work the stitches between * and * to turn again, 1 sl st. Next, work **ch 3, and in the 3 sc of the previous row work dc3tog, ch 3, 1 sl st in the top of the dc3tog, ch 3, 1 sl st in the next sc of the previous row** six times in all. Ch 3 at the end (which will serve as a button loop) and work the other side of the bracelet in the same pattern. Cut the wire.

- Border: Go all the way around the bracelet in sc, using the red wire and the size D hook. As this wire is thinner, work more than one stitch on the corners—the loops at the tops of the points and the buttonhole. Cut the wire.

- After weaving in the ends, cut them with the pliers and flatten out the work, then sew on the button.

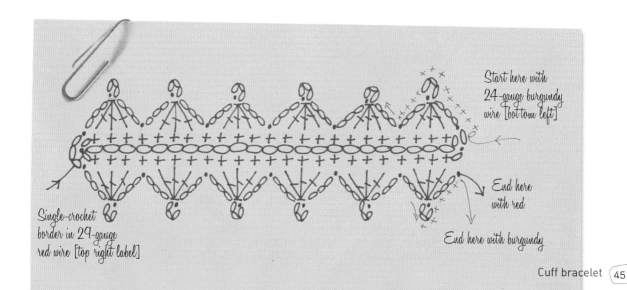

Start here with 24-gauge burgundy wire [bottom left]

End here with red

End here with burgundy

Single-crochet border in 29-gauge red wire [top right label]

Rosette bracelet

By mixing a bright or light color with black, you get a lovely marbled motif for this moldable bracelet.

Materials

1 spool of 29-gauge mint green wire

1 spool 24-gauge black wire

A button

Size D/3.25 mm crochet hook

Making the bracelet

- Make four rosettes following the stitch chart on the next page, crocheting with the mint green and black wires at the same time.

- Ch 6 and close it with a sl st to make a circle.

  Round 1: Ch 1, *1 sc, ch 2, 2 dc, ch 2* 4 times, 1 sc, ch 2, 1 dc, dc2tog.

  Round 2: Ch 1, 1 sc in the dc2tog of the previous row, *ch 2, 2 sc* 4 times, then ch 2, 1 sc, and 1 sl st to close the round.

  Round 3: Ch 1, then work all the way around the rosette in sc, working 1 st in each chain of round 2. Finish with 1 sl st to close it. Cut the wire at about 6 in.

- On the fourth rosette, at the end of round 3, turn and make a button loop: ch 4, skip 1 sc of round 2, and work 1 sl st in the next st. Cut the wire.

- Flatten out the four motifs (see page 15). One flattened rosette should measure about 2 in in diameter.

Assembly

- Sew the rosettes together using the remaining ends of wires, making sure that the centers of the four motifs are on a straight line, and that the button loop is placed on an end. Sew the button onto the other end.

TIP: Crochet more rosettes: some from two strands of wire like for the bracelet, others from just one strand of wire and with a smaller hook, and still others from three strands of wire (with a larger hook). Then sew them irregularly onto a delicate ribbon to create a long necklace in the same spirit as the leaf necklace (see page 38).

Stitch chart for the rosette motif

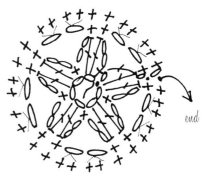

end

Accessories

Ring belt

Use more or fewer of these easy-to-make rings depending on where you like to wear your belt—at your waist or at your hips. This piece would also be ravishing in black or silver.

Materials

1 spool of 24-gauge tin-plated copper wire

85 in silver metalic ribbon, 0.6 in wide

Size E/3.5 mm crochet hook

Making the belt

- To make a ring, start with a chain of 16 sts and close it with a sl st to make a ring. Work in the ring obtained: ch 3, 1 dc in the first ch of the ring, then 2 dc in each st afterward. Close the round with 1 sl st in the 3 chains at the beginning. Cut the wire, leaving a short length for assembly.

- Make thirteen rings in all. In two of them, before you cut the wire, ch 4 and work 1 sl st in the second dc after the 4 ch to form a loop. Cut and weave in this wire.

- Flatten out the rings.

- Be careful that when you work the double crochets, you insert the hook through the chains in the ring, and not through the middle of the ring.

Assembly

- Sew the rings together, using the remaining lengths of wire, and making sure their centers are in line with each other and that the rings with loops are on the ends. The length of the finished belt should be about 33 in.

- Cut the ribbon in two pieces; fold each piece in half and slide it through one of the end loops in a fringe knot (see page 41).

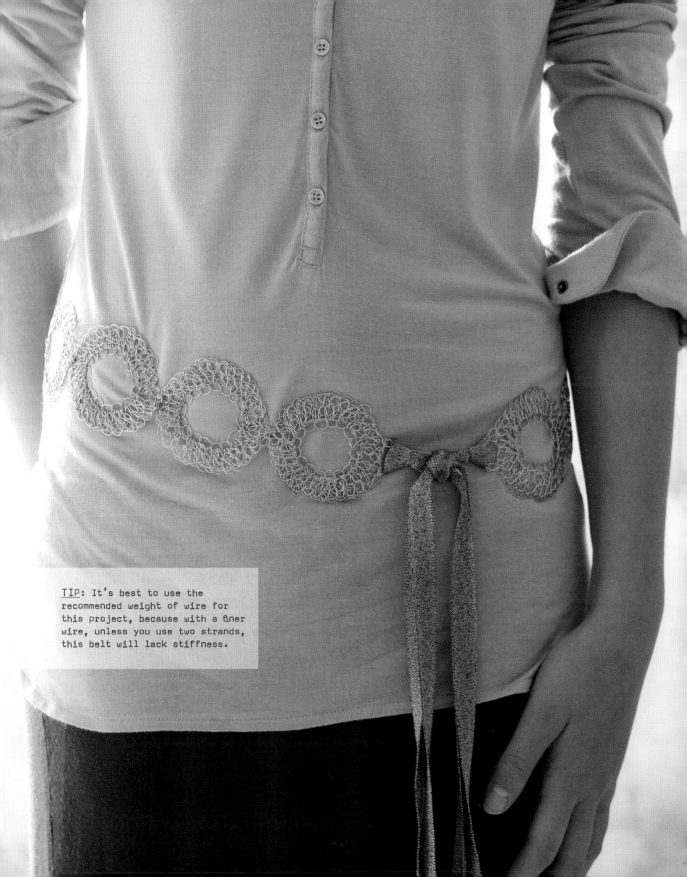

TIP: It's best to use the
recommended weight of wire for
this project, because with a finer
wire, unless you use two strands,
this belt will lack stiffness.

Two-color square belt

These bicolored squares make a trendy belt that will dress up a pretty dress or tunic top, even the simplest ones. It's also beautiful in black and in silver.

Materials

1 spool of 24-gauge black enameled copper wire

1 spool of 24-gauge annealed brass wire

A bit of black pearl cotton

2 buttons

Size G/4.00 mm crochet hook

Making the belt

- This belt is made with thirteen squares, but you can make it with fewer or more, depending on how you like to wear your belt.

- Starting with a loop (steps 1 and 2 from page 21), crochet squares using the pattern from page 36, but stopping after the first two rounds.

- Seven squares have the first row in brass and the second row in black, and the other six have the colors reversed. Cut the wire at the end, leaving a short length for assembling the belt. Cut and weave in the end of the inner wire.

- Flatten out the squares.

Assembly

- Sew the squares together, using the remaining ends of wire, alternating the placement of the colors. The length of the finished belt of thirteen squares is about 33 in.

- In the middle of the outer edge of the first square to the right, make a button loop from the pearl cotton. Sew a button onto each end of the belt.

- Another option is to close this belt with a ribbon, like the ring belt (see page 50).

TIP: It's best to use the recommended weight of wire for this project, because with a finer wire, unless you use two strands, the belt won't be sturdy.

Pearly handbag with disks

Pearly circles float softy from this purse, playing with color and light.

Materials

1 spool 29-gauge mint green wire

1 spool 29-gauge champagne wire

1 spool 29-gauge pink wire

1 spool 29-gauge lavender wire

2 pieces of cloth, about 12 x 16 in, one marbled (for the outside), the other plain (for the lining)

Narrow ribbon or flat shiny lacing that matches the cloth

Sewing thread

Embroidery needle

A bit of pearl cotton in a matching color

Buttons that match the cloth

Size D/3.25 mm and G/4.00 mm crochet hooks

TIP: You can also close the purse with a snap on the inside. Other arrangements and sizes of circles are possible--play around with it!

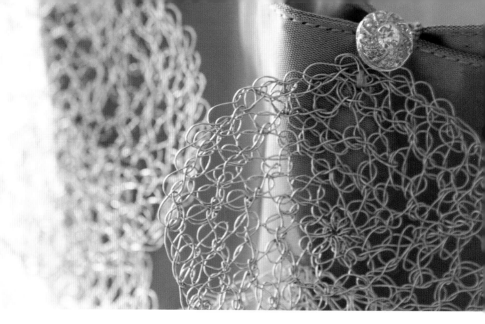

Making the circles

- In each of the four colors of wire, crochet with the size D hook three circles of 5 rounds in sc, working through the back loop of each stitch and following the explanation on page 63.

- Cut and weave in the ends of the wires. Flatten out the circles.

Assembling the handbag

- If your circles are 2¼ in in diameter or smaller, cut from each of the fabrics a rectangle 8 x 13½ in, adding ½ in on each side for the seam allowance. If your circles are larger, cut proportionately larger rectangles.

- Attach the circles on the front side of the purse, following the diagram on the opposite page. Start with the first row of lavender circles, attaching them to the cloth with a small stitch at the top of each circle. Following the line upward, next put on the pink circles, partially overlapping them over the lavender ones. Then attach the champagne ones, and then the mint green ones.

- Fold each of the two rectangles of cloth in half, right sides together, lining up the edges, and sew around the sides (be careful not to sew through the crocheted circles). Cut the two corners on the diagonal to remove the extra fabric at these points and open up the pockets. Turn the marbled pocket inside out and slide its lining twin inside it. Turn the top edge of the two pockets down ½ in and pin it in place. Set this aside for now.

Handle assembly

- With the size G hook and with all four wires together, ch 100, then flatten the chain out. It should be about 24 in long. Using a needle, thread the ribbon or lacing through the gaps in the chain.

- Slide the ends of the handle between the lining and the outer layer of the purse, on both sides of the project. Tack, then sew all the way around the opening of the purse, right below the edge. On the back, in the middle, make a loop with the pearl cotton and sew the button on the front.

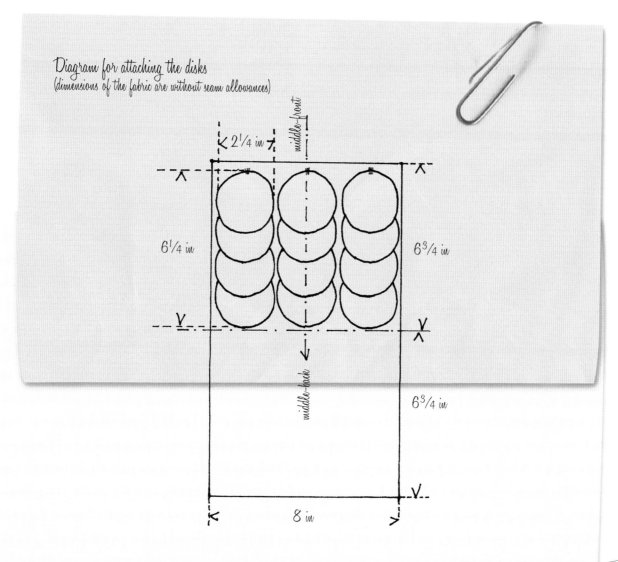

Diagram for attaching the disks
(dimensions of the fabric are without seam allowances)

Precious wire-mesh handbag

Very easy to make, this heady little jewelry bag will accompany you to your evening parties.

Materials

1 spool of 26-gauge dark green enameled copper wire

40 in of matching green cord, 0.2 in in diameter

Red velvet cloth

Fine moss green cotton cloth for the lining, about 12 x 16 in

Embroidery needle

Size G/4.00 mm crochet hook

TIP: If you want to make this purse in other dimensions, always start with a chain whose length is a multiple of 5, then add 2 more ch to turn (don't count the stitches for turning as part of the first row).

Choose whatever fabrics you want for the outer pocket and for the lining: bright-colored cloth, prints, and so on.

Making the handbag

- Ch 37 + 1 to turn and crochet 2 rows in sc (working through the back slope of each stitch) = rows 1 and 2 of the mesh. Next work rows 3 and 4 of the mesh (see the stitch chart on p. 60) 5 times, then finish with an extra row of sc through the back loop of each stitch, for a total of 13 rows. The rectangle you end up with should be about 9 in wide and 5 to 6 in tall and will form one of the two sides of the purse. Cut the wire, leaving a good long length for sewing the pieces together.

- To make the other side, go back to the underside of the chain you started with and work the 13 rows again, working up from the chain in the opposite direction. Cut the wire, leaving a good long length for sewing the pieces together.

- Flatten out the rectangle obtained.

Assembling the handbag

- Cut from each of the pieces of fabric a rectangle the same size as the one you crocheted. Add ½ in all the way around each of them for the seam allowance. Fold them in half, lining the sides up, and sew around the sides; trim the bottom corners on a diagonal and open up the pieces. Turn the velvet pocket right side out and slide the lining inside so that the wrong sides of the two materials are together. Fold over the top edge of the two pockets ½ in to the inside and tack them together just below the edge.

- Fold the crocheted rectangle in half around the bottom of the purse (the starting chain) and sew the two sides together to form a pocket. Slide the velvet pocket inside and sew its top edge to the mesh pocket using a sewing machine (or by hand if you don't have a machine).

Assembling the handles

- Make a knot in one end of the cord, leaving an inch or so at the end; cut it to the desired length for a handle, and then make a knot in the other end in the same way. Make a second identical handle. Sew them at the top of each side, wrapping the cord with wire for about an inch above the knots, inserting the wire through the crocheted mesh as you wrap it to attach the handles to the bag.

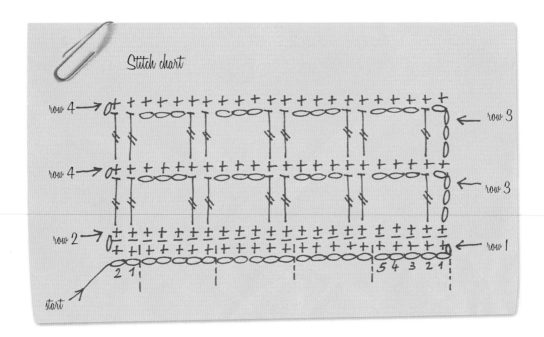

Stitch chart

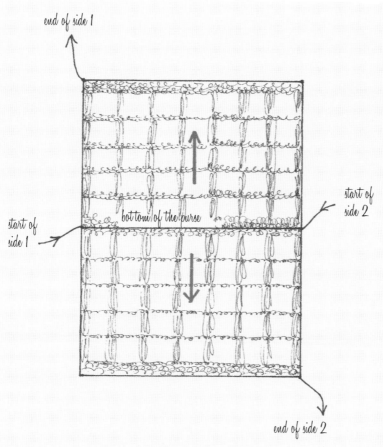

end of side 1

start of side 2

bottom of the purse

start of side 1

end of side 2

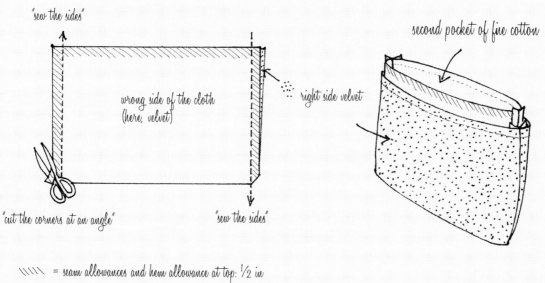

"sew the sides"

wrong side of the cloth
(here, velvet)

right side velvet

"cut the corners at an angle"

"sew the sides"

second pocket of fine cotton

\\\\\ = seam allowances and hem allowance at top: ½ in

Three-dimensional flower

On a barrette or a headband to
wear it in your hair, or on a
brooch to attach it to a hat
brim or a scarf, this little
flower is sure to charm.

Materials

1 spool of
29-gauge orange
varnished wire

A bit of natural
raffia

A barrette or a
pin back

Size B/2.00 mm and
D/3.25 mm crochet
hooks

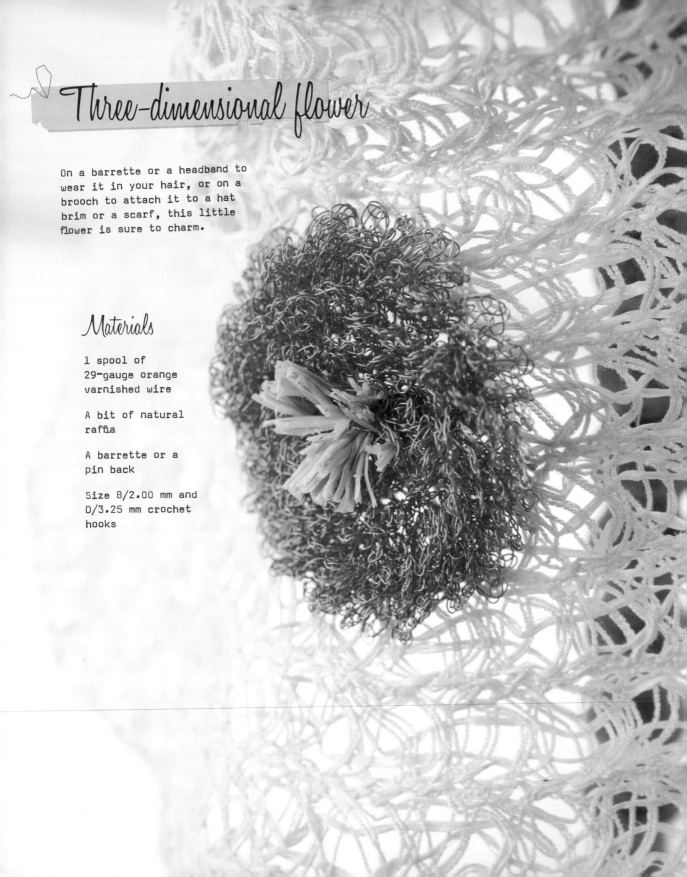